A Year & A Day

Memoirs Of A Regular Girl

AYANA BEAN

Copyright © 2021 by Ayana Bean

All rights reserved. No part of this publication may be reproduced, distributed or transmitted in any form or by any means, including photocopying, recording, or other electronic or mechanical methods, without the prior written permission of the publisher, except in the case of brief quotations embodied in critical reviews and certain other noncommercial uses permitted by copyright law.

ISBN: 978-0-578-98723-1
LCCN: 2021923235

Although the author and publisher have made every effort to ensure that the information in this book was correct at press time, the author and publisher do not assume and hereby disclaim any liability to any party for any loss, damage, or disruption caused by errors or omissions, whether such errors or omissions result from negligence, accident, or any other cause.

Adherence to all applicable laws and regulations, including international, federal, state and local governing professional licensing, business practices, advertising, and all other aspects of doing business in the US, Canada or any other jurisdiction is the sole responsibility of the reader and consumer.

Neither the author nor the publisher assumes any responsibility or liability whatsoever on behalf of the consumer or reader of this material. Any per-ceived slight of any individual or organization is purely unintentional.

The resources in this book are provided for informational purposes only and should not be used to replace the specialized training and professional judgment of a health care or mental health care professional.

Neither the author nor the publisher can be held responsible for the use of the information provided within this book. Please always consult a trained professional before making any decision regarding treatment of yourself or others.

For more information, email:
info@msyanabean.com

DEDICATION

I give honor to God from whom all my blessings flow. I also want to give a heartfelt thanks to my family and special loved ones near and far, who are my biggest cheerleaders and selfless supporters in all my endeavors. Your support has contributed to my fight to become great, and I am forever grateful.

This book is dedicated to all young girls and women who feel unworthy, desperate, and alone. I hope my story will cause you to make good choices in spite of difficult circumstances.

ABOUT THE AUTHOR

Ayana Bean hails from Boston, MA. At an early age, she noticed the difference between where she lived and where she was being educated--and vowed to make a better life for herself. Ayana's ventures led her to events headlined by Billboard, BMI, and ASCAP. Ayana soon became a vital music presence in Boston and worked as the regional liaison for several major record labels including Def Jam, Sony, Eone formerly Koch Records, and Interscope. However, the battles in her personal life--which consisted of raising two young sons, and the disease of drug addiction in the home, led her down a path of fiscal ruin.

In 2005, Ayana went to state prison for committing financial fraud. In 2013, she was convicted of financial fraud for a second time--but this time against the federal government. Ayana currently works independently in the music business. She is an advocate of at-risk women and gives talks to those in or transitioning from prison. Ayana's life is chronicled on the
American Gangster: Trap Queens Series on **BET**.
Her career in music, crimes against the government, and ultimate redemption will be told to the world in the series and in her new book A Year and A Day.

Contents

Introduction 2

Chapter 1: It's A Wonderful Life 5

Chapter 2: Love & War 9

Chapter 3: New Normal 15

Chapter 4: Silence & Abuse 20

Chapter 5: No Place To Belong 29

Chapter 6: Teenage Years 34

Chapter 7: Boys & Motherhood 39

Chapter 8: Suicide Attempt 45

Chapter 9: Independence 52

Chapter 10: Gunshots, Prison & Addiction 57

Chapter 11: Take The Bad With The Good 64

Chapter 12: Jail 71

Chapter 13: The Aftermath Of Jail 80

Chapter 14: Old Habits Die Slow 85

Chapter 15: Caught 90

Chapter 16: A Year & A Day 95

Chapter 17: A New Day 100

Conclusion 103

Introduction

Poverty, single motherhood, and homelessness are some of the social factors that lead to the rising number of women in prison. Women in prison have experienced victimization, unstable family life, and substance abuse, which has led to poor decision-making. Patience, faith, and wisdom from the lessons learned, can lead to a brighter tomorrow.

My friends call me Alice in Wonderland because I always tried to escape the painful realities that were both controllable and uncontrollable. Being sexually abused at an early age, birthed a silence inside of me that lasted until my young adult life. Music helped me to drown out the pain of abuse, violence, and dysfunction. My love for music and the music industry was my escape from reality. However, I had no escape when my decisions caused me to be locked up and sentenced to A Year & A Day in Prison.

I am Ayana Bean, and I am telling my story of going from the darkness of prison to the shining light of a businesswoman. I want to help women avoid poor decisions that can lead to imprisonment and motivate the women currently in prison who may feel trapped internally. I want to encourage women and girls to be patient with themselves, and to let them know that choosing the right thing to do, is always the best thing to do.

CHAPTER 1

It's A Wonderful Life

"If you're walking down the right path and you're willing to keep walking, eventually you'll make progress."

– **Barack Obama**

Between 1915 and 1970, my mother's and father's families were amongst the more than six million African Americans who moved from the South to the Northeast and Midwest. My mother, the oldest of eight children, was born in Birmingham, Alabama. My grandfather didn't want to raise his family in the South because all of the hangings and racism made it an unsafe place for black people to live. Consequently, my grandparents migrated to Boston, Massachusetts, after Dr. Martin Luther King Jr. was murdered, and the riots became unbearable.

They moved to Boston because it was better for Black people, and they thought it would help my grandfather find work easier. When they moved to Boston, they lived in various places, but they spent a lot of time in the East Boston projects where my mother met my father. My father, the oldest of 11 children, was born in North Carolina, which is the part of the south that his family migrated from. My mom and dad grew up together. Both sides of my family lived in the projects, and they were all friends.

I was born in 1974. My parents got married after I was born. My family left East Boston and moved into another project called Academy Homes. Having a close family bond was always instilled in me; they always told me that family was all you had, and that's where your blood, sweat, and tears went.

The Golden Child Era

For a long time, it was just the three of us: me, mom, and dad. I was an only child, so I got so much attention. I was also the first grandchild and everybody's favorite. I remember one of my favorite uncles would always have me hanging out with him and one of his girlfriends. It was as if I was the "golden child."

When I was five years old, my sister Shani came, and my parents got a place in Jamaica Plain Projects. My mother went to school and worked, and my father did the same. My family was happy, and I felt the love, especially from my dad. When my mother was working, it would be me, my dad, and my baby sister. Those were great times.

When I was in the 2nd grade, some inner-city kids in Boston, where I lived, were sent to suburban areas to attend school in better districts. We were in a program called METCO and the suburb that I went to school in was located in Sudbury, Massachusetts.

My favorite part about going to school was my ride to the bus stop. Neither of my parents had a car, so my dad would ride me on his bicycle. He would put me on his bike, ride me to the bus stop, and I would take the bus to school. If it rained, then he would put me on the handlebars with a trash bag over me to keep me from getting wet. My dad would also crack jokes on the way to the bus stop. I loved being with my dad so much that one time I intentionally used the bathroom on myself so I could stay with him. He was so mad at me, but I was still daddy's girl.

CHAPTER 2

Love & War

When I was around seven or eight years old, things began to change. I began noticing different things about my dad. He was laid off from work, he was on drugs, and he started cheating on my mom with other women in the projects that she knew. Consequently, my parents started to fight a lot. As a child, I didn't understand what was going on, but I was angry with my mother for fighting with my father. He was everything to me, so I couldn't understand why she was causing these problems.

Things got so crazy when one day I stayed home from school, and my dad had one of the women they were arguing about over. They were in the room while I was playing with my dolls. When my mother called to see how our day was going, I answered the phone after my dad told me not to. So when she asked what my dad was doing, I let her know that he was in the room with the other woman.

"What?!" she yelled. Once I reconfirmed it, she hung up. When my dad came out of the room, I let him know my mother called.

"Mommy called," I said to him.

"I thought I told you not to answer the phone," he said. In my mind, I'm like, well, I forgot, I am only a child after all.

"What did you tell her?" He asked.

"Well, I told her the lady was here borrowing something," I shrugged. My dad was so mad that I had told on him. The lady left. My mother came home shortly after, and they had one of the biggest fights ever. The fight was so bad, I felt like he hurt my mom.

My mom survived the fight. However, after this experience my dad became so abusive to my mom when he was mad or high on drugs. This was the beginning of my unstable life and the beginning of my anxiety.

"Research supports that depression, anxiety rule breaking, and aggression can be a behavior of a child who experiences his parents disagreeing regularly."

– (Brown)

The Fighting Era

Watching people fight was a normal part of my childhood. My dad fought my mom, my dad's girlfriends fought my mom, and my grandparents fought my dad. Watching those fights did not do anything to me physically, but emotionally I was scared. It was terrible to watch my parents fight one another, but it was even worse to watch them fight other people.

Mom & Dad's Girlfriend Fight

There was always something going on in the projects we lived in. However, I never expected to see this. If this fight had happened today, then this would have been on Youtube, Facebook, and Instagram.

Imagine this, I came home and found my mom rolling on the ground fighting a woman that my dad was having an affair with; Everyone was standing around watching. My friends were watching, some of my friends' mothers were watching, and many other people who lived in the projects were also watching. Then, the woman's other family members started running towards the fight and I was so scared. I yelled for them to stop fighting, but that did no good. All I could do was stand there and cry because I was scared that the other woman's family members would jump in and hurt my mom. Thankfully, they did not. However, I was embarrassed, but most of all I was so scared.

Dad & Grandparents Fight

My mom's parents were very involved in church, and they raised me the same. I learned how to pray, but I stopped praying because one time I prayed for my dad to leave, and he did. At first, I thought my parents fighting was my mother's fault, but then I thought it was my fault because I prayed.

One time, the fight between my parents was so bad, that my grandmother, my grandfather and uncles showed up at our house. My grandmother took me in a back room, so I knew something bad was going to happen. "We are going to stay here, but everything will be fine," my grandmother said to calm my anxiety as she locked the door behind us. All I could hear was my grandfather and uncles fighting with my father. I was trembling in fear. The amount of fear I had was unbearable, but things got worse.

After the fight, my father told me that he was leaving. I didn't want him to leave me so I became hysterical. He begged my grandmother to talk to me and explain everything as he said goodbye. I thought, this is all my fault. In my mind, my dad wasn't leaving because of all the fighting, he was leaving because I prayed for him to leave so that he wouldn't hurt my mom.

I was so torn and confused. I wanted my dad to be around, but I didn't want to see my mother hurt like that again. I wondered, was I helping my mom by praying for my dad to leave? Or did I pray the wrong prayer? From this point, I blamed myself for my dad not being around and that was so hard for me. I thought God listened to me pray and then He took my dad away. Therefore, I stopped praying all together.

CHAPTER 3

New Normal

The Dark Side

My dad was gone now, and it was me, my baby sister, and my mother. Although my dad wasn't in the house anymore, it still didn't stop the fighting. Back then, it was like a woman was her husband's property, so there was no support for my mom to keep him from coming over. She got restraining orders and other things in place, but it didn't stop him from showing up uninvited.

My dad would come banging on the door, and my mom would call the police but that did no good. The police would ask my dad to take a walk around the corner, but he would just come back. My dad became so persistent and would not stop harassing and fighting my mom.
One time my dad had my Godfather knock on the door for him. My mother said to my Godfather, as we looked through the peephole together, "If he's out there with

you, I'm telling you I'm calling the police. I'm serious, I don't want him near me."

It looked like it was only my Godfather standing there, but my mother still reiterated, "I'm telling you if I open this door and he's out there, then I'm calling the police." I knew my mother was scared, but she didn't want to believe that my Godfather was setting her up. After all, he was someone we all knew and trusted. Therefore, she trusted that he wouldn't bring any harm to her. However, we lived on the second floor, so when my mother opened the door for my Godfather to come in, my dad came running down the third-floor steps and pushed his way through the door.

My dad started fighting my mom, and I remember hating my Godfather for what he did, and as a result, I started to hate my father.

Before this fight, I was so confused, and I hated my mother. I didn't understand what she was going through as a wife and a mother. However, this fight taught me that my mother wasn't keeping my sister and me from our father; My mother kept us from his toxic behavior, and she was protecting herself. As I got older, I realized how dangerous the situation was.

At any of those times, my mother could not have been alive. I felt so bad for her that she went through that form of abuse because, to this day, it still affects her. It would be years before I would be able to spend time with my dad again. I would go by his parents' house looking for him, but I wouldn't find him. He eventually moved down south and later back to Boston. I wasn't able to have a relationship with my dad until I was a teenager. I missed him so much.

The Bright Side

After my dad left, I spent a lot of time with my maternal grandparents. My grandparents purchased a house. They bought a massive house that had a backyard, and all my family was always there. I also had friends in the neighborhood who would come over; My grandparents' house was my favorite place.

My grandmother spoiled me, so I always wanted to be with her. She worked at night. When I would spend the night at her house, my grandfather would pick her up in the morning, and she would come home and cook breakfast for everyone.

When she would arrive at the house after work, I would be upstairs with my two aunts. I thought one of my aunts was so mean because her rule was that I had to wait until she woke up to go downstairs to see my grandmother. However, I didn't let anything keep me from her.

As soon as I smelled the food, I would find a way to sneak down to see her. I would slide out of the bathroom and run down the stairs into her loving arms. I wanted to be with her and my grandfather all the time. I would cry when my mother came to get me, and it was time to go home. After my dad left, spending time at my grandparent's house was the happiest time for me.

CHAPTER 4

Silence & Abuse

Have you ever imagined feeling disgusting and unattractive? In addition to my parents getting divorced, there was something that happened to me that changed the way I view myself. What happened to me made me feel alone, but in actuality, I discovered it happened to many children.

"500,000 children will be impacted by child sexual abuse per year."

– (YWCA)

House

I would go to a family friend's house, and I would enjoy playing a game called, *House* with an adult who lived there. Even though I was playing with an adult, I thought it was fun because we were playing a game and after all, I was only a child. When we began playing House, I was about seven years old. It started out being me and an older male adult, but later on, a girl cousin around my age started playing too.

When it was me and him, we would go play upstairs at the family friend's house. Once inside the house, we would go all the way up in the attic, and then into our secret place, which was a closet. I didn't know it was wrong, but I knew it was a secret because he referred to the closet as a secret room. No one else knew we were up there.

While we were in the closet, he would molest me. He would take down my clothes and fondle my body parts. He would then show me his body parts and show me how to fondle him. This was our game called House.

Is This Wrong?

Although no one knew what he was doing to me, one time another adult called for me while we were up there. I went running down to see what she wanted. "What are you doing?" she asked as she saw my pajamas all the way open. I said, "Just playing." The other adult never investigated further.

One time, I mentioned the game House to a friend. Her reaction made me think that maybe I shouldn't be playing this game. However, he was loved by everyone so I thought it must be fine.

I developed some confused thoughts followed by negative emotions from these encounters of sexual abuse. First, I thought it was something fun to do. Then, it became less fun, and then, my cousin joined the game, and it became even less fun.

Now that it was three of us playing House, he gave us roles. My cousin was the mother, and I was the child. When my cousin got to be the mother and I had to be the child, I thought something was wrong with me, that I wasn't good enough to be the mother. In my mind, the mother was the most important person in the family. The mother was smart, beautiful and in charge just like my mother and my grandmother.

Therefore, when my cousin was chosen to be the mom, he was the dad, and me the child, I felt like I was less than. I thought he chose her to be the mother because she was more developed than me, and because I was more of a stick figure. This left some scars with me because I felt like I wasn't good enough. The sexual abuse went on between the ages of 7-9, but the internal conflict would have lasting effects.

After learning more about my body and that only doctors were allowed to touch it, I now knew it was wrong for sure. I told my family, but they didn't listen to me. I was an imaginative child who talked to her dog and things like that, so I think that's why no one believed me. There was nothing left for me to do because back then we learned to not tell business outside the house, to be secretive and not talk about anything going on in the house, out of the house. This caused me to develop a lot of resentment towards my family members.

> *"Believe them—very few allegations of child sexual abuse are false."*
> **– (YWCA)**

Although my family members didn't believe me, I felt worse because one of them insinuated that it was my fault. After the incident occurred, one day I was sitting on my grandfather's lap. My grandfather was and is an awesome man whom I've always adored. However, when I was sitting on his lap, an adult in my family said, "You see what you are doing? You know what you are doing, so you better stop." I was too young to completely understand. However, I was old enough to recognize that she was trying to blame me for what he did. This was confusing to me because I wasn't sure if she was blaming me or not. I wasn't sure if she believed me or not.

The other adults may not have believed that I was being molested, but I made sure that my sister and younger cousins believed me! I made sure they didn't trust "The Adult" enough to be alone with him. I became overprotective of them to protect them from experiencing what I did. I always talked about it to my younger sister and girl cousins so that they wouldn't be trapped into playing *House*. Although my family didn't believe me, The Adult ended up showing his predatory ways by getting a young girl pregnant.

> *"93 percent of children who are victims of sexual abuse know their abuser."*
>
> **– (YWCA)**

Not This Time

The Adult was the first, but he wouldn't be the last to try and sexually abuse me. One day I was walking from the bus stop. Normally, my grandad would pick me up, but on this day, he wasn't there yet. Therefore, I started walking hoping that I would run into him.

It was so hot this day and it got even hotter for me because I had on a shirt and a stupid itchy sweater. As I was walking, I noticed this guy behind me. I recognized him, but I didn't think I knew him. However, he looked like a leprechaun man with evil eyes and a bumpy face, so I started walking fast.

I walked faster and faster, but he yelled,

"Yana! Slow down, I'm gonna walk you home."
I froze a little bit and I couldn't really breathe.
I wondered; *how did this man know my name? Walk me home? How does he know where I'm going?* Then I realized this was a friend of The Adult. I started running even faster, and he started chasing me. He was getting close because I could feel his heavy breath on my neck.

"Come here Yana!" "I know the game you play!" he yelled. I thought to myself, "Is he talking about the game I used to play with The Adult? Who told him?"
At this point, I could see my family's house, but I couldn't find my voice to scream. As I began to find my voice to scream, he grabbed my arms and started dragging me into the woods on the dead-end street. I finally found my voice and I screamed, "HELP! HELP! Get off of me!"

Knowing that the adult probably marked me based on the game of House we used to play, now that I knew better, I was determined not to let another man sexually abuse me.
I was screaming, kicking, scratching, and hitting the man.
"Shut up!" he said.
He was so strong, and I was a small 4th grader, but I bit him as hard as I could, and it worked! I got away! I started screaming and I saw him run the opposite way. By now, I had peed myself right through my stockings,

but I made it to a relative's house without this man sexually abusing me.

Silence

When I finally reached the relatives house where my family was. I said, "This man tried to take me in the woods!"

"What are you talking about girl?" someone asked.
I was talking fast trying to explain what happened, but I felt like nobody was listening. I thought to myself, didn't they see my clothes? My shoe straps around my ankle? My ponytail out of place? The dirt on my clothes? Couldn't they tell that something happened? Why doesn't anybody ever listen to me? Can they hear me? I was devastated. I learned a big lesson. I learned to keep quiet because nobody was going to listen to me anyway. I wished I could talk to my dad I thought, but "Where is he?" I cried on the inside.

The Dark Side

"Child sexual abuse can have lifetime impacts on survivors— especially without support. It can impact educational outcomes, lead to heightened symptoms of posttraumatic stress disorder, higher suicidality, drug abuse, higher likelihood of teen pregnancy and chronic health issues." (YWCA)

On top of the internal pain from all the fighting with my parents, family members and my dad's girlfriends, I now had to deal with the remnants of being molested, attempted sexual abuse, and no one believing me. I thought, this can't be life. From this point on, I went through a lot of changes, and I had so many insecurities. I felt unheard, ignored and unhappy.

I didn't stay silent about the abuse and attempted abuse, although no one believed me. I hope my story will help other girls still tell someone anyway and not stay quiet if sexual abuse is happening. I hope my story will also encourage mothers not to be so willing to leave their children with friends or family members.

"Child sexual abuse is a crime that happens across race, religion and class and has lifetime effects. It includes any interaction between a child and an adult (or another child) in which the child is used for the sexual stimulation of the perpetrator or an observer. Child sexual abuse is often predicated on silencing the victim, and as a result, reporting and disclosure is low."
(YWCA)

CHAPTER 5

No Place To Belong

"Divorce in and of itself, and with children, is devastating."
– Robin Wright

Shortly after my parents divorced, and I was molested, my mom, my sister and I moved out of the projects and into another neighborhood. I had friends that lived in this neighborhood, and two of those friends went to the same school as me in the suburbs. I loved living there because some of our other family lived near us, and it wasn't as bad as living in the projects. However, where we lived was devastatingly different from the nice suburb, I went to school in.

I wondered why I needed to go across town just to get a good education and I became frustrated with the disparity between the two places. I went to school in this lovely place where everyone lived in nice homes and had great jobs. After school, I went home where I still lived in the "hood," my friends were in the "hood," and my life reflected the "hood."

Going to the school in the suburbs gave me an experience that introduced me to another possibility of life. Still, I couldn't understand why inner-city families weren't given the same education. What were they learning so differently in the inner city that we had to go to the suburbs to receive an education? Why couldn't the inner-city schools mirror the schools in the suburbs? Was the school preparing us for the real world or did we live in the real world? The main thing the school couldn't teach us was how to survive in our "hoods." I felt like I was living in one world by day and another by night.

> *"You can't underestimate how traumatic divorce is for the children."*
>
> **– Isla Fisher**

Even though we were in a new house, I found myself alone and I wanted my dad. One day, my father tried to come over to visit our new house, and he was drunk when he came. My mom didn't want to let us outside to see him, but she felt safer with family living there, so she let us go out in the hallway and talk to him. During the visit, he became verbally abusive to my mother, so she ended that visit, and I didn't see my dad again until I was a teenager. I never hated my dad for not being there because I still felt I prayed wrong.

As I was adjusting to our new place, change happened again. My mother moved on with another man, and she had someone new that she loved. Both my mother and father grew up together with this man, so everyone was familiar with each other. As a kid, wanting all the attention, I felt like I was losing out. I was also against my mother's new relationship because it wasn't my dad. My younger sister adjusted better, which made it easier for him to have a relationship with her. However, I was missing my father, so it was more difficult for him to have a relationship with me. My mom and sister formed a family with this new man. I felt like I wasn't a part of this new family and didn't fit into their happy ending. I felt like he treated me differently. While the three of them had matching Adidas sneakers, I would have some off-brand sneakers.

When I was 10 years old, my mom had a baby and gave me another sister. I was distraught. Before she was born, I wrote my mother a letter and told her that I didn't want her to have a "yellow man's baby," that's what I called him, and I told her how I hated him.
I felt alone and upset, but writing letters made me feel better. I wrote letters to my mom and grandmother. Writing was a good outlet for me to release the pain because it made me feel like I wasn't talking and being

ignored by others. I was also a creative and articulate kid, so I used to write letters to express myself. I have notebooks full of poems and literature, and it felt good to get my feelings out on paper. I used that as a form of someone listening to me because I felt I was shooed away, and no one wanted to hear anything from me. Writing and listening to music is what I turned to when I felt excluded from my mother's new family, and I wanted to escape the feelings of not having my dad around.

CHAPTER 6

Teenage Years

"While many kids seem to adjust fairly to their new living arrangements and can revert to their daily habits, some children just can't.
– (Smith et al.)

My father wasn't around, my mother had a new relationship and new baby, and I felt like my mom was taken away from me. Everything bothered me.

I now had two sisters and my younger sister's dad was the new man in my mother's life; He made her happy. I was happy she was happy, but I resented her at the same time. I loved my sisters, but I was also jealous of them because I felt like their life was good while mine felt like it was incomplete without my dad. I knew I was missing something in my life.

I began to act out because it was such a difficult time for me. Life felt lifeless, but I loved to skate. My friends in the neighborhood who went to the same school as me were the ones who introduced me to skating, but my mom wouldn't allow me to come off the porch. I used to beg my mother for days to go and she finally started giving in when I was 13.

There was a skating rink called *Chez Vous* that we would go to on Friday nights. Every neighborhood would be skating there from Dorchester to Rockberry. I loved it because it was like a big fashion show in the 80s. The boys who had the money and all the girls would be there, it was kind of like the club for us.

I loved going to Chez Vous. First it was couples skating, and then they would allow us to open the dance floor. My favorite thing about skating was the music and dancing; I loved music and dancing. My only problem was that my mom wanted me to be home by 11pm, which was when dancing started getting fun.

As I got older, I understood why she didn't want me to be out until it was over because it was dangerous. Not so much inside of Chez Vous but after it was over, which was after midnight, at the let out. The issue was some people wouldn't actually come skating, but they would come to the let out, which caused all the drama and fighting to start. It became dangerous because there would be fights involving different people from different street gangs, and there were even some stabbings.

During this time, I also started liking boys and there would be so many boys out on Friday nights skating. I wanted so badly to be a part of the party life and I loved the music and dancing, so I would break my curfew and not listen to my mother.

I was 13, and the kids I was around were 14-16 years old and I was trying to be a big girl despite not being ready for that. I tried to smoke cigarettes and I hated it, but I was trying to be cool. I was also trying to drink beer even though that wasn't what I wanted to be doing either. I was a rebellious young teenager trying to make myself feel better about my life, but I made some bad choices. This became the beginning of my poor decisions leading to unwanted consequences.

I had gotten myself a boyfriend and thought I was grown. I remember I didn't come home one night because I was hanging out with him, my girls and his friends at 1:00 am. I was scared to go home. I wasn't trying to stay out that night, but we were all hanging out and running the streets. This caused a lot of problems between my mother and I.

I loved the street life and the people I was around felt like an escape from all the confusion in my head and missing my dad. I started hating going to school in the suburbs because my friends were in other schools. I felt like I wanted to be a part of their world. Going to school in the suburbs was a disconnect and I hated it as a teenager. It was a different language, different culture and all-around different atmosphere. Running the streets seemed fun at the time and I didn't know how to make sense of things. It was a difficult time for me. Consequently, the street life gave me many unwanted circumstances, spankings from my mother, and it ultimately gave me my wish of switching schools from the suburbs to the city with my friends.

CHAPTER 7

Boys & Motherhood

Now that I was a teenager and I liked boys, many boys started noticing me. To me, it was cool to not care about boys but to get the jewelry, money, and anything else I wanted from them. It made me feel important like I was something more significant than what I was. I got all this attention and gifts from boys in the street; we called them "D-Boys." I also learned that when you hang around with trouble, then trouble will find you.

Drugs & Money

Where I hung out, it was common to see people use and sell drugs. Although neither one I did myself, I still hung around the sellers and benefited from their dealings. My piece of the action was big door knocker earrings and bamboo rope chains. I even had a car that one of the boys bought me.

The turning point for me was when I was dealing with a guy, and he had a problem with a couple of other guys. I walked to his house one day, and a couple of the guys he had issues with spotted me. They started to walk fast to catch up with me. I didn't know what was about to happen, but I felt like no one would touch me or anything like that because I had nothing to do with my boyfriend's dealings.
"Where is he?" They walked up to me and asked.
"I don't know," I replied.
"Well, we just left his house, and he wasn't there,"
"I don't know; I'm on my way over there," I said again.
No sooner than those words left my mouth, the bigger one of the two snatched me up, threw me into the brick wall, and pulled a gun out.
"If I find out you knew where he was, I'm going to kill you. I could kill you right now, actually," he said, putting the gun to my cheek.
"You don't have to do that bro, put the gun down; she has nothing to do with it," his friend stepped up and said. By this time, I was crying hysterically, and I almost pissed my pants.

The guy with the gun ended up taking all my jewelry, and I was so scared I didn't even care. I later got my jewelry back from the guy who defended me, and I later found out he liked me. However, I was scared straight after that, and I didn't want to hang with anybody who had anything to do with the streets. I realized being around people like that was dangerous.

I started back focusing on going to school and thinking about my future. However, by this time, I had skipped school too much and I missed a lot of schoolwork. I had a meeting with one of the guidance counselors, and I was kicked out of the METCO program. I was sent to an alternative school in Boston to get my points up. After I got my points up, I enrolled in Boston public school in the inner city. Although I didn't like what I saw, I was finally able to see the difference between the schools in the inner cities vs. the schools in the suburbs.

Now that I was in the school in my neighborhood, I couldn't find many who were planning for their futures; There weren't a lot of people talking about going to college. I thought about owning a hair salon, but I couldn't get any information, and I also didn't want to be another black girl doing hair. I was able to land a job and work at a bank for the last two summers of tenth and eleventh grade year. I thought I could find a promising career in banking, but I got pregnant in my last year of high school. Thus, I still graduated from Boston Public Schools.

Beginning of Motherhood

Although I was embarrassed to be a pregnant teenager, I was also happy because I thought I would have a family again. My grandfather was the last to know that I was pregnant because I was ashamed. He was like a father figure to me, so I never knew how to tell him. I was so small carrying my son, he didn't notice. The day I had my baby was when he found out I was pregnant. Despite not knowing, he was still there for me, and he supported me. I still feel bad that he was the last person to know but the first person there to support me.

I had a lot of complications during my pregnancy. Being young and not taking care of my body caused me to develop preeclampsia. One day I wasn't feeling well. I had blood clots and some form of a stroke. I blacked out and when I woke up, I had a baby. I had to have a C-section. My son was born five months premature, and they didn't think he was going to survive.

My son was in three different hospitals and had a long road ahead of him. He was on life support, an incubator and then once he got better, he went into a rehabilitation center. I knew that God would take care of my son and I never once believed the doctors. This is when I learned to trust God and put my faith back in Him.

If I would've known what I knew now, then, I would've taken my pregnancy more seriously. Despite what they said about my son, he surpassed all expectations. He was never underdeveloped or behind in school. I was happy to be a mom. I felt like having a family would feel that void of what I was missing from my family.

CHAPTER 8

Suicide Attempt

*"Divorce can turn a teen's life upside **down** in many ways, so it is important for parents to look for signs of depression in teens. And they **have to be aware of the emotional consequences.**"*
– (PBH)

I was now out of high school and trying to figure out the direction my life was going to take me. I had hopes of starting a family with love and joy. However, it wasn't long before I discovered that some of the challenges my mother faced in the past, I was now facing. The only difference was, I wasn't as strong as my mother.

My boyfriend/child's father began turning more to the streets, while I was turning towards making sure my family was stable. In addition to having one baby, we had another baby on the way. I still lived at home with my mother, but I wanted a place of my own; I was determined to become independent. Because I was pregnant with my second child, I felt it was necessary to leave my mother's house and get my own space with a solid foundation.

Without the means to leave on my own. I made a plan to go into a shelter so that I would qualify for Section 8. I found out that I could get emergency housing if I was in an environment deemed unfit to the state. Although my mother's house wasn't that bad, I still felt like I would try my luck. When the inspector from the shelter arrived to inspect my mother's house, he immediately found joint roaches lying in the ashtray.
"That's an immediate placement, we can get you out of the house today," he said.
"Today," I said. "Yes," he replied and told me the procedure. I was completely shocked.

The Grass Isn't Greener

The decision to go into the shelter was a poor one on my part. I thought my oldest son and I were going to the shelter immediately; However, we were shipped out to a motel on the outskirts of Boston. I remember rubbing my growing belly that night while laying with my son praying that this shit worked. I was at the motel for about 2 ½ -3 weeks before they found a women's shelter for us to go too. I was escorted to a Catholic Shelter for women, and it was an eye-opening experience. I felt like I was locked up. I couldn't go anywhere on certain days, I had to do a meeting every day for an hour and I even had to clean up after other women. "How long am I going to have to be here?" I thought about it every night. I was in the shelter for about two months.

I went to the shelter because it was a way for me to get financial assistance and gain independence from my mother. However, the grass was not greener on the other side. I would go and spend days at my mother's house to escape the shelter. This made me depressed. My child's father was missing in action, which was becoming usual for him. I was stuck pregnant making a way on my own with my partner. I was so miserable, and I took it out on my mother. I was at odds with my mother because I needed someone to blame for the mishaps that were happening in my life, so she was an easy target.

I felt as if I could give my mother the guilt trip and make her feel bad. However, this didn't make me feel better. In between being at odds with the two important people in my life, being in a shelter and everything up in the air, I felt like I wanted to be free from everything.
The perfect life that I dreamed of was not turning out like I pictured it. The fighting and cheating that I watched my mom go through, I was now going through the same thing. After I gave birth to my second son,

things still seemed to be going downhill. It was the same thing every day. I couldn't stand the loneliness or the constant fighting daily. I got so fed up that I attempted to commit suicide.

"Suicides among young people continue to be a serious problem. Suicide is the second leading cause of death for children, adolescents, and young adults age 15-to-24-year-olds." (Aacap)

One day I had an argument with my son's father and my mother. I had two arguments in one day with two important people in my life. The arguments weren't that serious, but it was the last straw for me. I was fed up. Deep down I didn't want to die, I only wanted the noise to stop and the pain to go away. I bought Dimetapp, which is like Benadryl.

I decided to take the pills and I felt like if I wasn't here, it would be better for everyone because it was a constant fight. I took six or seven pills and took my kids to my best friend's house. When I got to her house, I told her what I did, and I started feeling sick to my stomach. The room started to spin, and I could no longer hold my balance.

"Ayana, are you okay?" I heard.

"Take my kids," I said as I attempted to catch my fall but passed out on her living room floor. I wasn't completely out immediately because I could feel my body being lifted onto the stretcher and people around me talking. However, when I arrived at the hospital, I was unconscious. I woke up to machines beeping around me, tubes hanging out of my mouth and down my throat.

"Hello Ms. Bean, I'm Doctor Evans, we are going to remove the tubes." A tall Indian doctor said, after he removed my tubes, they gave me water to soothe my irritated throat.

"Ms Bean, due to the nature of the situation we are going to keep you for a few days for observation. We were able to pump your stomach and remove the pills you ingested."

"Okay," I said with a hoarse voice.

"I need to ask you a couple questions. Is that okay?"

"Yes,"

"Did you really want to kill yourself?"

"No,"

"Why did you take this pill then?" he said and I didn't answer.

"Are you living in danger?"

"No,"

"Okay, your vitals look good as I stated we are keeping you for a few days and then you can go home to your family."

"Okay," I replied, and he walked out. I couldn't help but to think how stupid my decision was because I felt even worse after my suicide attempt than I had before.

The next day my partner, (the children's father), came to see me. I was happy to see him, hell, I loved him despite his infidelities and his addiction to drugs, which we will later go into more details later on. When he walked in, he had such a look of disgust on his face.

"Why would you do some dumb shit like that?" he asked.

"Because of you and life," I thought. But I kept my mouth shut, he was a big reason why I wanted to be exact.

"That was so stupid, did you think of anybody else when you did that?"

"HUH!" He yelled, causing me to jump but still I remained silent. He wasn't nurturing me like someone he loved, trying to end their life. Like the mother of his children wasn't laid up in a hospital bed. He was the love of my life and I figured I was his, so how could he be so aggressive at a time like this?

"You know what, I wish you would've died," he said, getting up and walking out.

I let the silent tears fall down my cheeks, having someone that you love wish death on you can change your heart in a way you wouldn't imagine. Those words shattered my heart into pieces, but the worst was yet to come.

CHAPTER 9

Independence

"Instead of letting your hardships and failures discourage or exhaust you, let them inspire you. Let them make you even hungrier to succeed."

– Michelle Obama

I wanted so badly to be independent and on my own. I saw the shelter as a means to get Section 8. However, I still ended up back where I didn't want to be, my mother's house.

I left the shelter and moved back to my mom's house after feeling like I had stayed in the shelter long enough and still didn't receive Section 8. I knew that I had to figure out a solution because raising my kids in a shelter was totally against what I wanted. My goal was to provide a stable environment for my kids, so I decided to get a job in the daytime, and then I got another job in the evenings. I began working hard to save for a house.

During this time, barely in my 20's, the relationship between my partner and me wasn't good. I grew up normalizing things that shouldn't have been considered normal, so my toxic relationship with my children's father was familiar. However, I continued to be optimistic about my family.

Within a couple of months of leaving the shelter and going back to my mother's house, my partner and I decided to be roommates with some of his friends in an apartment. It didn't make any sense because they lived a different life than we did. It also wasn't good for us because our relationship wasn't solid enough due to his cheating. Against my better judgement, we moved in with his friends anyway. No sooner than we moved in, I found out he was cheating and bringing a girl over while I wasn't there. That was all I needed to move back to my mother's house, again.

As time went by, I started to get stronger, and I realized some things I needed to do. While I kept working so that I could provide for my family, I also began researching and talking to some of my coworkers about moving into an apartment outside the city. They told me that the rent was $500.00, which I was excited about because I didn't know it was that cheap.

"You should move into my apartments," my coworker said to me on lunch break at my night job with the phone company.
"How much are you paying?" I asked.
"$498.00 a month," she said.

The next day I went down to her apartment building and filled out an application. Within a month, I was approved for a small townhouse without a cosigner requirement. This was a sense of relief because I wanted so badly to have my own house with my boys, and I finally achieved my goal.

I packed up my stuff, and I left my mother's house yet again. I wasn't concerned about my partner or how anyone else felt. When my income tax refund came, I purchased a small car as well as bunk beds for my kids. I threw the bunk beds on the hood of my car, tied them down with some rope, and made my way to my new townhouse. I didn't care about my bedroom; I wanted to ensure my sons had everything they needed to live comfortably. I had wall-to-wall carpet, so I made a pallet on the floor until I could afford to buy my mattress. Nevertheless, I was grateful that we had a place to call home.

> *"Do not bring people in your life who weigh you down. Trust your instincts, good relationships feel good, they feel right, they don't hurt."*
>
> **– Michelle Obama**

When I moved into my new place, my partner still lived in the other apartment with the roommates. I told my partner that we had our place and then two days later, he moved in. I never asked him if he was still involved with the girl he cheated with. I brushed it under the rug; I assumed everything would go back to normal.

What was normal, I never would know. He wasn't home enough, and I felt I needed him home more. This should have been a huge sign, but sometimes when we are trying to clean up other people, we miss the red flags. I continued to work harder, and all he did was stay in the streets; We fought more in our place than we had before. My love for him was so strong and ran so deep that it outweighed logic.

CHAPTER 10

Gunshots, Prison & Addiction

"Love is patient, love is kind. It does not envy, it does not boast, it is not proud. It does not dishonor others, it is not self-seeking, it is not easily angered, it keeps no record of wrongs. Love does not delight in evil but rejoices with the truth. It always protects, always trusts, always hopes, always perseveres. Love never fails."
– (I Corinthians 13: 4-8 NIV)

I was now 23, and the year was 1997. My partner and I were still living in our place trying to make ends meet. One day I turned on the news and my heart dropped. My partner had been shot in the neck at a festival and his face was plastered across the TV. I was shocked and scared. One of our friend's mothers came and got me and took me to the hospital. When I got there, I learned that along with being shot, he was being detained in the hospital because he had a gun on him at the time he was shot. He survived the gunshot wound, but he didn't come home because he was sentenced to a year in jail based on the gun charge.

Before my partner was shot, I was working as a financial advisor, and I still had to pass the Series 7 test for my job because we sold insurance. We had a certain amount of time to pass the test. The week after he got shot, I took the test and I failed. I was now jobless and on my own with my children.

Although I didn't have a job, I still felt a sense of relief that my partner wasn't home. I didn't want him to be in jail, but I was relieved of the stress he caused. I didn't completely write him off and I did take the kids to see him in jail, but I wouldn't stay the whole time. However, he got into a fight and went in the hole, so I never took my kids to visit him again.

While he was in jail, I began discovering more and more of what I wanted. For me, that was when the partying began, and I started going out and living my life. I was partying and drinking every weekend. My mother and my sister would take turns watching my kids and when my mom got tired, I would have my sister come and stay at my house with the kids. Even though I lost my job because I didn't pass the Series 7, I was still able to take care of the kids, take money to my partner in jail, maintain my household, and go partying. My partying days came to an end when my partner had about two months left in his prison sentence; It was fun the 10 months that it lasted.

Then you will know the truth, and the truth will set you free."

– (John 8:32 NIV)

When my partner came home from prison, he began hanging out in the same area he was in before going to prison. The area that he hung out in was known for people using drugs. Before he went to jail, I knew he smoked weed, but I suspected he was smoking something else because of the way he would nod out. I knew about crack, cocaine and weed and his behavior wasn't consistent with any of it. However, I would eventually be in for a rude awakening.

I was at a popular club I always went to with my cousin. This guy I knew, who also had a crush on me for a long time, started with his usual neighborhood gossip. I didn't know the information he would give that night would be so devastating.

After the club he walked over to the car and we started having a discussion, "Yana how's everything going? You know I heard your boy doing what he's doing," he said.

"What do you mean? What is he doing?" I asked.
"You don't know, your boy uses heroin?"
"No, he doesn't, stop lying,"
"Yes, he does, everyone knows about him."
"You are such a liar! Don't ever lie on him again!" I yelled and we pulled off. As soon as we pulled off, I called my partner and told him what the guy said.
"Honey, do you know this guy lied and said you do heroin?! I can't believe he would lie like that to my face and in public. I should have kicked his ass!"

I yelled, ranting and raving. I noticed that he sat silent on the phone and didn't say a word. He didn't get mad, he didn't even say anything. When it finally registered to me, I dropped the phone.

"Oh my God no," I whispered, covering my mouth.
How could I not know that this was happening? Was I so detached from things that I didn't pay attention? How could I be so stupid? My mind was racing a mile a minute. I was thinking about my health, his health and my kids. I couldn't stomach finding out he was a heroin addict. I didn't know what I was going to do.

Eventually, the same pattern in my life happened again. We couldn't keep up with the rent. I lost yet another job and we no longer had a place to live. I believe we could've gotten help, but my partner no longer wanted to be there, so I think that contributed to his lack of effort. For me, it was back to my mother's house, and he went to his mother's house.

Now that I knew what was going on with him, I started noticing things I didn't before with his addiction. I felt stuck and lost because I didn't know what the future held.

I got another job and started taking college courses to better my future for my children and I. I was still worrying about my relationship that clearly; I was the only one in. I didn't think he had an interest in making it work. On my end I was still trying to make it work and find solutions to the problem. I helped him get into rehab and in the beginning he was willing. However, over the years it became a back-and-forth thing. This became our life for 20 years, he would get clean, come home and do it all over again.

"Above all, love each other deeply, because love covers over a multitude of sins."
– (1 Peter 4:8 NIV)

I think that my love for my partner outweighed the love I had for myself and that's something till this day I am working on. Some people will judge how you love someone and how they react to your love. I know first and second hand that it's hard to watch someone you love fight an addiction especially when you have children with them. I thought back to how my parents were when I was growing up, and once again, I noticed it was very similar to what I was going through with my partner.

It felt like I was becoming a bag lady carrying so many bags that weren't mine for so many years. It also felt like I was a janitor, normalizing and cleaning up situations that I shouldn't. I wished I had the kind of life as the women who lived in the suburbs where I went to school. On the other hand, my reality was I came from a dysfunctional family with drug abuse, and I was living the same life. However, for my children's sake, I was determined to make it better.

CHAPTER 11

Take The Bad With The Good

"You have to take the good with the bad, smile with the sad. love what you got and remember what you had."

– Chime

In the early 2000s I caught my first break. I started working at this company that was helping families to get financial aid to get into school. I was making good money, and I also finally got approved for Section 8. I was headed in the right direction, but my partner's addiction led me to do things that would change my life for the good and the bad.

Strength

My boss was so impressed by my work ethic, I was asked to go to other colleges to help them complete and sign the paperwork for financial aid. While going to the colleges, I learned there was an opening at Emerson College School of the Arts and it was a better opportunity; I interviewed and got the job.

I was the new Director of Student Financial Services, and I was in charge of making sure that the funds and payments were received for the student's tuition, and I was also in charge of the *Perkins* loan processing. That loan came from the bank for the student's tuition and any funds left over was distributed back to the school. When checks would come into the office, I would stamp them and send them on their way. My job was great, and I also began taking advantage of the free courses at the school I was able to.

I was also interested in music and magazine publishing, so I started taking free classes at the school I worked at to learn the business. In addition, some friends of mine were starting a record label, so I connected them to the radio station at the school. This was the beginning of me planning events in the music industry. This led to me planning big music events and I thought these events were what I wanted to do in the future. I was enjoying the life I was creating.

Threat

My partner and I were still living together. He was still on drugs, so he was taking everything that came in. One month, rent, lights, gas and the rest of the household bills were due. My partner had gone missing along with the money. I didn't want to lose my place and I also had my children's livelihood to consider. Therefore, I had to find a solution to fix it.

I was at work processing checks when a light bulb in my head switched on. *"I can just take a check and when I get paid put it back,"* I thought. These were checks from the bank sent to the college. It was loan consolidation. The students would get a loan for their education and the bank would send the money to the school. One day I took a check for a little less than $1,000 and put it into my account. I didn't think about the negative consequences I would face if something went wrong because I was desperate. The next day, the check cleared, and I couldn't believe it. I took the money out and paid my bills for that month. I got excited, my thought process was I can take another check and pay it right back. However, I kept doing it every week. Over time, it went from $1000 to $12,000 dollar checks.

Opportunity

Money was no longer an obstacle for me. I was living a good life and still cashing those checks. I had so much money in my bank account, and I felt complete. It was all about the freedom that money bought me. No one knew what I was doing, it just looked like I had a great job and things were finally looking up. My goal was to get well known for putting on events in the music industry, and it all started happening. I was in close proximity with known record executives and celebrities, and I became a popular resource in my city for upcoming artists. I was enjoying my life.

I would sneak out with my sister and children and go wherever my heart desired. I would leave an envelope with money under my partner's pillow so that he could be straight while I was gone. You couldn't tell me anything. I was at big events in V.I.P. with some of the biggest names in the game. One of the first events I attended was "TJs DJs." TJs DJs was a record pool, which was known for breaking records for artists in the South. I was interested in learning about record pools and how you got albums on radio. I decided to call and inquire about being involved with TJs DJs, and I actually spoke to the organizer and his partner. The event was in Tallahassee Florida and I flew down to meet them. I was actually in the room with shot callers; My dreams were starting to come true. I was jet-setting all over the world and I decided it was time to buy a house.

I began the process of buying a home, I took the first-time home buyers' program, and I wasn't worried about how I would pay for it. I was spending the money I was stealing, and my checks from work were just piling up. My sister was in college and pregnant with twins and we decided to go look for a house with enough room for us all. The first house I looked at I fell in love with and bought. My partner didn't know I bought a house, and he didn't know the money I was touching.

"I bought a house, and we are moving in 30 days," I told him one night after I closed the deal.
"How can we even afford that?" he asked. "It's not as hard as you think. Just know I did it and we are moving," I said keeping it brief.

Weakness

After the house purchase cleared, I started getting nervous because my bank account was heavy. I had close to $150,000 and I knew I had to leave that job, or I wouldn't stop taking the money. I felt like this was my own personal rehab that I was putting myself through. I felt like if I left then I wouldn't want to steal anymore. I switched to another job where it had nothing to do with checks at all. A few months later I was at this new job, but it was something in the back of my mind I felt like I didn't do to cover my tracks; I couldn't put my finger on it. It didn't take long for those thoughts to become reality. It was auditing time for the new school I worked at and some detectives came and asked me questions. I thought they were asking standard questions for the audit, but then I realized it was much bigger than that.
"So, tell me what happened when you were at Emerson?" They asked.

I was so confused but I knew that I was caught. I wanted to throw up, but I held it together. I never knew this day was coming, but I knew there was no way to escape it. They handcuffed me and took me out of the building. I was grateful that they tried to make it as unnoticeable as possible. However, by the time my feet hit the pavement outside, all my bank accounts were frozen.

"Always forgive, but never forget, learn from your mistakes but never regret. People change, things go wrong, but just remember life goes on."

— **Chime**

CHAPTER 12

Jail

"Faith is not trying to believe something regardless of the evidence. Faith is daring to do something regardless of the consequences."

— **Sherwood Eddy**

I got caught doing something that I knew was wrong. No one knew what I was doing, and no one other than myself was responsible for my actions. Although it was not easy, and all of the money I saved was gone, I accepted the consequences of my actions.

One Phone Call

"Can I have my one phone call please?" I asked the C.O. The C.O led me to the phone, and I called my sister.
"Hey, I'm in jail." I said to my sister when she answered.
"WHAT!? WHAT JAIL? WHERE ARE YOU?!" she screamed through the phone.

"Hold on let me ask. Excuse me Sir, where am I?" I asked the C.O. When he told me, I let my sister know so she could come and get me.

When I asked the C.O what my bail was he told me $12,000. I was devastated because all my accounts were frozen. I didn't have anything outside those accounts, and I didn't think my family would come through for me. I had no idea how the hell I was getting out of jail. My sister went to the state trooper's office, and they let her know that I had no choice but to go to court.

Court

The next day I went into court and my entire family was there. My hopes were high seeing everybody because I assumed they banned together and got the bail money. I knew at least 12 people had a stack a piece, but when I saw my sister, we read each other's minds. She shook her head no and I knew they all had come empty handed. On one hand, I was so thankful for the support, but on the other hand I couldn't understand why nobody came with bail money.

Once I left the courtroom, I was transported back to the holding cell eating the bologna sandwich they gave me; I was devastated. I was being transported to National Street City Jail. When I arrived, I walked into my cell and had to change my clothes. Before they closed the cell, I asked for one phone call.

"You got one more phone call before you go upstairs to the population," the C.O said. There was no way I was going upstairs. I was a tough cookie up until she told me I had to go upstairs. I tried my last call, and I called my cousin. "Please... I'll pay you back, can you please come get me?" I asked, crying to my cousin. My cousin was babbling and asking a bunch of unnecessary questions, and then his wife grabbed the phone.

"Ayana, where are you?" she asked me. Once I explained everything and how I was stuck, she grabbed her purse and was on her way. I got on my knees and thanked God. I was grateful for my cousin's wife, and I always will be. "My cousin said she's coming so I don't have to go upstairs," I told the C.O. I sat in that chair quietly for hours not bothering anyone until she came and got me. I went home and faced a financial crisis because I had a new home, and a new mortgage with no money. Despite going through everything I put my faith in God. I always believed in God and I stopped praying when my parents were going through rough times, but now my prayer life was strong.

Guilty

My next court date came, and I didn't ask for a trial. There was no point, there was a paper trail leading to me. All I wanted to know was the time I was facing. I wanted to prepare my family for my departure. Although I focused on faith, I was extremely depressed so I would take Tylenol PM to stay asleep. I tried to be as normal as possible for my kids and keep the game face on. I was after all their only parent around at this time.

Letters about past due payments continued to come in, so I knew I had to get a job. I ended up getting a job at another college and I was able to catch up and get on a payment plan. I put on a music conference and contacted labels to add more income. I also continued to help local artists to make ends meet. I was still creating a name for myself without anyone knowing my situation. It involved participation from major labels such as Def Jam and Bad Boy. I also included independent labels. I was able to sit at tables with major labels and have major discussions.

Sentencing

After the success of the conference, I plead guilty to the charges. I received six months in the state prison and received three years' probation. For the crime I committed, I expected five years, so I was grateful. With my sentence I was allowed to tie up affairs because I had small children at home.

I lied to my children and told them I was going to a women's conference for six months. I taught my children the things I knew, and I didn't want them to know the truth. My children were at home while I was away with their father. I left three months of mortgage payments behind and with the help of our family, he took care of the household. Thank God he was clean during this time.

I went to South Bay Correctional, and I waited to be transported to the facility. I prayed for my family more than anything during my sentence. I prayed that I didn't get into trouble during my bid. There was an artist I helped who was also in jail. We couldn't see each other because we were on separate sides, but I could hear him. He spoke life into me and with his words of encouragement I faced the sentence with faith that I would make it through.

Jail Life

I was scheduled to go to New Man, which is the first unit you enter into the prison. People usually spend a few weeks in New Man, then you get classified and assigned to whichever unit you will spend your time. Although you are supposed to be in New Man for some time, I was immediately sent into the population where I would do my time. A C.O. I went to school with was shocked I was there and so were the other inmates who

knew who I was. I made the best of my time by reading and educating myself. Not everyone was for me, but I treated everyone with respect.
Within the first couple of nights, I went through hell. I remember one night in my sleep I heard water running. I couldn't shake the feeling of hearing water. When I finally opened my eyes my bunky was sitting on the sink with her legs wide open urinating in the sink. I couldn't believe that the sink I was supposed to brush my teeth in was getting urinated in. That is when the sober feeling of being in jail hit me. I called home every couple of days to let my sons know that the "women's conference" I was at was going great.

After the sink incident, everything started to be smooth sailing. I didn't link up with anybody or have any tight friends. We had a choice to go to the library or gym. Majority of the time I would choose the library. The one time I chose the gym I learned that that's the time where people would hook up. I learned very quickly to stick to the library.

My time wasn't that bad. I was being looked out for, so I would look out for my bunky's. After all, I am a woman of God. I became cool with one in particular. She could not read or write so I was helping her read and write letters to her family. I got into an altercation with her because she was having a hard time one day. I am not a back-and-forth girl, so I simply stopped talking to her and stopped looking out. I ended up getting my room moved because I knew that she would continue to try me.

Over the next couple of days, she got some bad news about her son and needed my help. In that kind of environment, she had disrespected me so for me to speak to her or help her wasn't going to look good on my end. You had to develop a certain behavior in jail, so I ignored her.

A couple days later I heard what happened to her son and I made her a care package. I left it at the door for her without saying a word or letting her know it was from me. She got into another altercation and was being moved to another unit. Before she moved, she came to my door and walked over to me.

"I just want to tell you that the worst thing I could've done while in here was disrespectful to you. You've been good to me," she said. I continued to give her the cold shoulder. I started seeing so many bloody prison fights and it never sat right with me. I would always think *"Damn, this is just like TV."* After that I went to church on Sundays and chilled in my cell. I barely came out to eat because of the food they served. After two months, they let me know that I would be released. Counting down those last few days was hard but I thanked God because in total I did three months. I was incarcerated in January and free in March.

CHAPTER 13

The Aftermath Of Jail

"All things work together for good to those who love God."
– (Romans 8:28 NKJV)

My grandfather was outside waiting for me on my release day. I saw his purple Lincoln Town Car from the window. I was so happy to see him and my grandmother. The best part of the day was seeing the joy on my children's faces when I surprised them by being at the house when they came home from school; That was a feeling I will never forget. Although I was happy, I wasn't out of the woods yet; I was on probation, I was losing my house, and I didn't have a job.

Probation

I was sentenced to three years of probation. I had to regularly check in with my probation officer and it was tough. I never liked people telling me what to do, however I had no choice but to follow the rules to

remain out of jail and home with my children. I did catch a break with my probation officer.
One day he said,
"You're going to have to do community service. It involves picking up trash on the highway."
"I'm not doing that. I can't embarrass my kids like that. What can I pay to not have to do that?" I asked.
"I won't make you do it for the sake of your kids," he replied.

I appreciated him for being understanding and sparing my kids the humiliation of watching me collect garbage, but my luck surely began to run out.

Out Of Jail, Now What?

As a woman going to prison and then coming home, my self-esteem was low. I didn't want my family or anybody to see me down so that they wouldn't feel bad for me. I felt I had to be strong, not just for myself, but also for my family.

When I came home from jail, I had only three months saved for the mortgage, and we were coming up on the fourth month. The good thing about this was it was around tax time, so I was able to file my taxes and get money. It lasted for a minute, but I needed a job, which was hard to find because I had a record.

I was losing my house because after those tax returns ran out, I needed a job. By the time I got a job I was too far behind to even catch up. My mortgage started off at $1100.00 and bubbled to over $2000.00 dollars a month. This was because I had a variable rate, and I could never fix it. Missing payments lowered my credit score so I couldn't get loans and things I needed with my credit.

I didn't know what I could do, I only knew my sons were graduating from this house; That was my driving factor. I got some help from my aunt and their father's parents as well. I was able to hold off, but the mortgage wasn't the only bill. I had a small footing, but it seemed impossible to catch up on everything.

"Fear not, for I am with you; Be not dismayed, for I am your God. I will strengthen you, yes, I will help you, I will uphold you with My righteous right hand."
– (Isaiah 41:10 NKJV)

I developed a fight in me. It kept me going regardless of the situation. I began working at a data entry job and tried my hardest for my kids not to notice a shift in their lifestyle. I was still trying to make moves in the music industry as well as work. I was on probation so I was limited on what I could do. During this time, I put together a second music conference. I could barely afford it, but I made it happen. When a shooting occurred at my event that was when I decided I needed to put it to rest.

Although I tried to protect my kids, there were a lot of things they saw and heard. We continued to struggle even after I found a better job. As a family, we got hit pretty hard. Thinking back, my poor decision of taking money resulting in me going to jail, made my financial situation worse than it was before I took the money. I wished I could change things and do it all over again, but my life would never be the same and it was up to me to fix it.

CHAPTER 14

Old Habits Die Slow

In 2009, three years had passed, and my probation was over. I was working a regular job, and I knew this couldn't be it. I knew I needed to do something to make more money because I wasn't living to my fullest potential.

There wasn't any growth at my current job, so I looked for a better one. I applied for a new job in Higher Education at a trade school as a financial advisor. I never lied on any application, and they didn't do a background check. They went strictly off my experience. I got the job, it was closer to the kid's school, and it had nothing to do with checks.

After going to jail due to stealing checks at a previous job in Higher Education, I was happy to get another chance. I was able to help students get into school despite them owing student loans. This job made everything more accessible, although I still wasn't making enough to make the mortgage work on my own.

Infidelity, Domestic Violence, and Drug Abuse

My home life never changed; I was still dealing with my partner having a severe addiction. My kids were getting older, and they started noticing dealers coming to our house for their dad. My partner and I fought more and had many altercations because of his cheating and drug use.

The fights got so bad. One battle resulted in us tumbling down the stairs after he was spotted with another girl driving my car. However, the worst fight happened when he started taking TVs out of the house to sell them. I was at war in my own home, but I was still determined to have both my children graduate while living in this house.

> *"Over 60% of imprisoned women are mothers of children under age 18."*
> **(The Sentencing Project)**

I learned about the company I was working for, and I also learned how to get extra money from it. It was similar to what I did ten years prior; it was another illegal hustle. I wasn't worried about my first jail sentence. I was focused on survival and doing anything for my family.

At this job, I took refund checks; after payments were sent for the school, most students didn't know they were eligible for refund checks. I discovered that when people requested their refund checks, the money would come back into the school. Once I figured what was happening, I used it to my advantage. It was on a much smaller scale than the first case. Once I looked through a student's account, and I saw they didn't request their refund, I would ask for it. It was really to make ends meet, but I traveled a lot more. I was funding my partner's addictions, my kids, my household, and my love for travel.

The extra money helped me to reach most of the goal to let the kids graduate from that house. My oldest son had graduated, and my youngest son was in his last year. I made my financial situation not as heavy as it should be. In reality, nothing was changing in my home life with my partner. It was too much, so I let the house go. We moved into an apartment near our old house. We went on with our lives until I was on a trip to the Bahamas.

I couldn't save my house, but I was still determined to enjoy life. I went on a trip to the Bahamas, and something wasn't right. I knew something was wrong in my gut because when I went to charge one of my many bank cards, it declined. I brushed the feeling out of my mind. Right after that, my son called me.

"Hey Ma, some federal agents are here to talk to you."
I later found out that I didn't tie up a loose end with a check. I figured it could wait until I got back, but a student called to inquire about their check. If I didn't leave early, I could have handled it, but I didn't. I couldn't help thinking that this was happening again. I knew exactly what was happening.

I was more scared now because the federal agents were looking for me. Even after I stole a quarter of a million dollars before, it still wasn't federal. This amount wasn't even $100,000, so I was confused. I boarded the plane to meet my fate, but this time I didn't know if I would make it out of this case.

> *"Women typically become incarcerated after experiencing gender-based trauma throughout their lives. About eight in ten have experienced domestic partner abuse. A large majority have survived sexual violence."*
>
> **– (APA)**

CHAPTER 15

Caught

I was caught. I accepted the responsibility that I did something wrong, and I was ready to face the consequences. From the trauma from my parents fighting and then splitting up, to being sexually abused shortly after, teen pregnancy, my own battle with domestic violence from a drug addict partner, serving time in jail, and now federal sentencing. This would be one of the toughest battles that I would face, yet I was determined to go through it alone.

I didn't tell anyone about the sentencing. When my mom or sister would ask me about it, I would change the dates and not disclose the actual date. Before my sentencing day, I woke up and explained to my kids about the next day. I made breakfast, prepared my kids for the day, and let them know I would be in touch.
I went to my attorney's office, and we talked about how the process was going to go. We went into detail about how long they would give me. Since I had a previous case that raised my guidelines points, they used that,

which put me up to five years in prison, so I didn't know what to expect. My attorney said he would ask for probation to start at a low end and work his way up if he needed to.

When the day came for me to be sentenced, I walked into the courthouse by myself. When I got there, I gave my ID, and the security guard said, "Wow, there's a lot of Beans here today." Bean is my last name, so when he told me he checked in many Beans, I was like, Oh my goodness.

My sister had found out about my court date and was there before me. When I walked into the courtroom, I saw my sister and my cousin. That brought me to tears because I said I didn't want them to come. In reality, I didn't realize how frightening this experience would be.

Sentencing

It was now time for me to learn my fate. I had already negotiated a guilty plea with the prosecution and the attorney. We didn't know what my time would be because, under the guidelines, it could be up to five years. After all, I had a previous case.
When it was time for me to be sentenced, I stood up to talk to the judge, and I took full responsibility for what I had done. I asked the court not to give me a heavy sentence. The prosecution wanted me to serve three

years, but the judge ordered me to serve one year and a day in a federal prison camp plus three years' probation. I now knew my sentencing time, but I didn't know where, how far, or when my jail time would start. My attorney asked the judge to let me have some time to get my family business in order before I started serving my time. The judge agreed.

The judge allowed me to self-surrender to the place I would be serving my time. I didn't know where that would be, so that wait-and-see caused me a lot of anxiety. I discovered there weren't any federal prisons in Massachusetts, so I thought I would go to New Hampshire or Maine. Nonetheless, about a month after sentencing, I found out I would be doing my time in Lexington, Kentucky. Kentucky was far from my family. The worst part about my sentencing time and location was that I was leaving my sons who were now growing into young men.

Single Motherhood

I went home and explained to my children what happened at sentencing. At this time, my children were two young adult males. My youngest son had just finished high school and was on his way to college, and my oldest son had recently graduated college. However, they were still young and needed my guidance and direction. The thought of leaving them weighed heavily on my heart.

My children and I were close, and we usually talked about everything with each other. I always tried to let them know they could bring anything to me and didn't have to hide anything. However, after my sentencing, they didn't express how they felt about me going away. Over the next few months, I was trying to figure out how my sons would be able to maintain themselves while I was away. I didn't know what they were thinking, and I wasn't sure they understood the scope of what would happen.

CHAPTER 16

A Year & A Day

I was sentenced to one year and one day in federal prison in Kentucky. To some, this may not seem that bad, considering it was my second offense. On the contrary, 12 months in a foreign place can be devastating. The judge gave me a few months to get my affairs in order; Some may have taken that opportunity to run. As for me, the agony of this experience taught me a huge lesson. My motto became, *the best thing to do is always the right thing to do.*

Surrendering

I bought myself a one-way bus ticket to Lexington, KY, on the Peter Pan Bus. My two sons and my youngest sister drove me to the bus station. It was probably the most silent we all had ever been and the most embarrassed I had ever been in front of my family.

My sons were sending their mom off to the bus station to travel to Federal prison to start the unknown. Before I got out of the car, we squeezed each other tight, and on the bus, I went. They sat in the car until the bus took off. I had to stop looking at them through the window because I couldn't hold my tears. I wanted to get off the bus and live a life on the run. Nevertheless, I had to do the right thing to put the wrong things behind me.

Prison Life

Two days after arriving in prison, I was able to get a job in the kitchen. Then a few weeks later, I got another job working next door in the men's prison, cleaning the offices. I felt good about working in jail.
I also spent my time at church every Sunday. I enrolled in a truck dispatching course, and I went to the gym every day, which was my peace of mind. Because I was far away in Lexington, KY, I didn't expect any visits, and I didn't get any.

While I was in jail, I used the time to be alone and focus on getting out. I struggled with the guilt and fear of not seeing my sons and praying they wouldn't end up in prison. I even worried if they would be alive when I got home. The fear of young black males on the street with one parent in prison and the other parent struggling with drug addiction was devastating enough. However, I focused on my day-to-day survival so that I could see them again. I followed the rules and kept myself busy with activities to keep out of any trouble in any way. I didn't hang out in groups; Jail was time I spent with myself.

The Bad Side of Jail

Prison is no place I would ever recommend anyone to go. My advice to women and young adults is, obey all the rules so that you never have to repay your wrongs with the entrapment of prison. Hence, there is no escape.

I witnessed fights between women who were dating other women in prison. There was fighting every week. I saw one fight where a woman slammed another woman's face into the marble staircase, and she lost her two front teeth. Watching all the fights in jail was devastating. Any chance to go out I would be out there running and walking the track and listening to music grasping for peace.

Time didn't go by fast at all when I was in prison. Each day seemed like a month. I kept myself busy by enrolling in classes, working two jobs, working out daily and reading the Bible. There is no bright side of prison. The only good thing about it was being able to focus on my relationship with God. For the first time, I read the Bible and for the first time I could understand the Word of the Lord.

I learned more about myself and what I needed to do with myself. The biggest thing I learned was that I never wanted to go back to prison and nothing was worth missing time out of my life and my children's'. The only good thing that came out of prison was that I made it out of there alive.

One Year and One day sentence is a 12-month sentence with credit for a good time earned of 56 days. I started my time in Federal Prison in January 2014 and was released to the halfway house in October of 2014. In November 2014, I was released from the halfway house to my mom's until January 2015.

CHAPTER 17

A New Day

When I came home, I had to realize that my boys were now grown men and I needed to respect them as the men they were and not consider them my little boys. My partner and I were still together, but we later broke up. It wasn't drug addiction that broke us apart. It was the neglect, disrespect, not coming home, loss of hope, and insecurity. These things had overwhelmed me. I felt like I was enabling him to keep making bad choices. It seemed that addiction kept winning over our family and I was defeated. My relationship with my partner ended in 2018.

From Pain To Purpose

After leaving prison, I received so many denials for job opportunities due to the background check pulling up my criminal history.

A few months after prison, I applied and started working at a women's fitness and spa center in early February 2015. I worked there for five years and received three promotions during that time. I worked there while filming *American Gangster Trap Queens* and continued to work there as the show aired. Once COVID hit in March 2020 the fitness world was put on hold and I no longer had a job. I was compensated by BET, so I had money to make ends meet and savings for later. I made smart choices while working and filming. I lived below my means and saved as much as I could.

The Right Thing To Do

After prison, I also aligned myself with organizations whose purpose was to support women in prison and women re-entering society after prison. I worked with State representatives to create and push for laws that support better treatment of prisoners and to uphold the rights of prisoners. It was this that motivated me to start my own Non-Profit organization to give back and do the work to support those imprisoned and being released.

I found a deeper connection with myself, I learned that it was ok to use the power I had to help others who couldn't help themselves. It's ok to be selfish to protect yourself from things that don't feel good to you. Protecting my peace and building my strength is what I am working on even now.

Conclusion

My journey has been a great learning experience for me. I didn't believe I was strong, but I was able to make it through abuse, shame, insecurity, and prison.

I started with ordinary dreams. I learned to braid hair in the 7th grade and had dreams of being a hairstylist. In high school, I started learning business finance and accounting, and I loved that too, so I figured I would own a business someday. However, I moved too quickly.

I craved independence, which brought on significant responsibility. When that got tough, I made poor decisions that were criminal. After making it through prison, I no longer think the same, want the same, or believe the same. I matured and was able to heal my internal wounds.

When I went through childhood dysfunction, abuse, and imprisonment, I felt like I wouldn't make it, but because I focused on myself, my faith, and my freedom, I believe I am successful today.

I was able to turn my past problems into positive actions. I decided to make a start by putting skin in the game. I started reaching out to city counselors and other organizations to see where there was a need. Lastly, I started my nonprofit organization, *A YEAR AND A DAY FOUNDATION*, a transitioning program for felons re-entering society. As a Philanthropist, I am now able to give back and make a positive difference.

I hope my story will help other women and men. I pray that my story will be used as a cautionary tale that can encourage others to have patience with themselves and always to know that the best thing to do is the right thing.

Works Cited

Brown, Jeremy. "5 Rules Parents Need to Remember When Fighting in Front of the Kids." *Fatherly*, 8 May 2019, https://www.fatherly.com/love-money/rules-parents-fighting-in-front-of-the-kids/.

Child Sexual Abuse Facts - YWCA USA. https://www.ywca.org/wp-content/uploads/WWV-CSA-Fact-Sheet-Final.pdf.

Smith, Sylvia, et al. "The Sad Truth about What Divorce Does to Kids." *Marriage Advice - Expert Marriage Tips & Advice*, 17Sept.2020, https://www.marriage.com/advice/divorce/what-divorce-doeDavis, Jeanie Lerche. "Teenagers: Why Do They Rebel?" *WebMD*, WebMD, https://www.webmd.com/parenting/features/teenagers-why-do-they-rebel.s-to-kids/.

"Father Absence, Father Deficit, Father Hunger." *Psychology Today*, Sussex Publishers, https://www.psychologytoday.com/us/blog/co-parenting-after-divorce/201205/father-absence-father-deficit-father-hunger.

Incarcerated Women: Poverty, Trauma and Unmet Need. https://www.apa.org/pi/ses/resources/indicator/2019/04/incarcerated-women.

"Why Are There so Many Women in Jail?" *Google,* Google, https://www.google.com/amp/s/www.thenation.com/article/archive/why-are-there-so-many-women-in-jail/tnamp/.

"Incarcerated Women: Poverty, Trauma and Unmet Need." *American Psychological Association,* American Psychological Association, https://www.apa.org/pi/ses/resources/indicator/2019/04/incarcerated-women.

CPSIA information can be obtained
at www.ICGtesting.com
Printed in the USA
FSHW021707141221